WORDS
FITLY
SPOKEN

WORDS
FITLY
SPOKEN

BY

BRUCE GOODPASTER

"A word fitly spoken is like apples of gold in settings of silver."
Proverbs 25:11

Xulon Press

Xulon Press
2301 Lucien Way #415
Maitland, FL 32751
407.339.4217
www.xulonpress.com

Printed in the United States of America.

ISBN-13: 9781545608432

Contents

When God Speaks

Open Your Heart

Walk With Him

Trumpet Sounds

Introduction

In 2007, I had a near-death experience and an encounter with the Lord that ultimately helped spur me on to advancing His Kingdom, in these last days, by writing poetry. Since my young adult years, I have been interested in how biblical prophecy is being fulfilled, and how current events indicate that we are living in the last days on earth before the Lord returns. Sensing the urgency of Christ's imminent return has brought a focus to my poetry that urges you, the reader, to listen when God speaks, to open your heart to Him, to walk with Him in faith, and to listen for the trumpet sounds that will signal His return. I pray that God's peace, which surpasses all understanding, will fill the hearts and minds of all who read these poems.

Bruce Goodpaster
April 24, 2017

"But without faith it is impossible to please Him, for he who comes to God must believe that He is, and that He is a rewarder of those who diligently seek Him."

Hebrews 11:6

Dedication

I would like to dedicate this book of poems to my Lord and Savior, Jesus Christ, through whom I have exchanged death for life and despair for hope. I owe special thanks to Carol Goodpaster, my wife of forty-five years, for using her English teaching skills to help edit and craft the layout of this book.

I also would like to dedicate this effort to our five children: Kirsten, Kellee, Kendra, Nathan, and Lindsay, and to their spouses. I pray they will share the hope that is in these poems and in Jesus Christ with their children and our grandchildren: Nile, Luke, Ella; Jacob, Meghann, Ben; Sarah, Isaiah, Rachel, Hannah; Emily, Bethany, Julie, Jonathan; Noah, Madelyn, Charlotte.

When God Speaks

The Divided States of America

In Peter Marshall's book, <u>The Light and the Glory,</u> he recounts how God intervened in the early years of our country by helping General George Washington and his army achieve victory over the British. It is an inspiring book that gives the reader an appreciation of how our young nation leaned on the Lord to protect them from defeat and lead them to victory; now, our nation appears to be divided. We must have God's help if we are to survive as a nation.

Our founding fathers trusted in the Lord with great vision.
They called upon God when making tough decisions.

Their rewards were great, as they sought Him for a solution.
God led them through many battles to win the revolution.

Young men gave up their lives in the quest to be free.
Though outnumbered by the enemy, they gained the victory.

"One nation under God" was the proclamation they lived by,
And they defeated the enemy as they sounded the battle cry.

There is much division in our nation today.
We have walked away from God, leaving order for disarray.

Many have been slain who love the Lord,
But the enemy has no chance against God's mighty sword.

We desperately need a revival in our land,
Because a house that is divided cannot stand.

God gave us the ministry of reconciliation;
Only through sharing Christ can we save our nation.

Acting Out in Faith

As I read in the book of Joshua, the nation of Israel had to cross the Jordan River to reach the Promised Land. God's instructions were to cast their feet into the water, before He would part the Jordan for them to cross over on dry land. They had to take a step of faith before God would perform the miracle. As we travel through life today, we are still put to that test. Do we place our hope and trust in Jesus in every situation? Or, do we come up with our own ideas, leaving God out of the equation?

Am I trusting in Jesus to lead me today,
Or trusting in myself to find another way?

If I don't act out in faith and choose what is right,
I will place myself in peril and surely lose the fight.

For we are in a battle every moment of the day,
I must take a step of faith, and He will help me choose the way.

Joshua believed in God and not in man's perception.
He trusted God and walked in truth, not led in the wrong direction.

Don't let your pride get in the way.
Jesus will lead you and tell you what to say.

Asking God to help may not always make sense,
But doing what you think is right would be a greater expense.

As you trust in Him and avoid the daily rubble,
He will give you peace in a world filled with trouble.

His plans are for good; He wants the best for you.
Listen for His still, small voice; He will tell you what to do.

It won't be long because the King is coming back.
Are you following Jesus and keeping on track?

Do I place my trust in Christ in every situation,
Or do I follow my own path, leaving God out of the equation?

Trust in the Lord

*In the world, there are many things that demand our time and effort.
Having a good job, a nice home, and car are things we think we need;
but true fulfillment in life only comes from Jesus Christ. He is the hope
for the dying world that we see all around us. In Him, there is true hope,
as we trust in Jesus for all things.*

When I wake up each day,
Jesus is there to lead the way.

He is my hope in a world filled with doubt.
He gives me joy; that's what life is about.

As I place my trust in the living Lord,
He gives me peace while others live by the sword.

There is a day coming when we'll see Him face to face.
Jesus is the only answer for the human race.

If you are feeling empty in the world down here,
Just look to Jesus; you have nothing to fear.

Look to the Savior who died for you and me.
He gave His life on a cross and set me free.

As He hung on the cross in agony and despair,
He asked God to forgive them; He really did care.

Do you struggle as to what life is about?
Reach out to Jesus; He takes away doubt.

Could Jesus Come Back Today?

We live in a world filled with hope and tragedy. As Christians, we need to be soldiers for Christ. Yes, we are in a war against the enemy, and we will win the war because God is greater than any power in this world. As soldiers, we need to be "battle-ready", getting our strength from the Lord. Read your map (the Bible) every day, pray, and ask God to lead you. As you cast all your cares on Him, you will find that He cares for you. He will lead you to victory as you trust in Jesus, who has overcome the world. Remember He paid the penalty for our sins by dying a terrible death on that wretched cross, so trust in Jesus, your source of strength.

Each day, we are closer to the Day of the Lord drawing near.
It will happen in a moment when our Savior will appear.

To take us home where we belong; it will be a glorious sight.
When Jesus arrives, He will take us up to be with Him alright.

We look around and see the trouble the world is in today.
Just as He said, there is strife and envy; it's created quite a fray.

So carry your cross and burn out bright, so people see Jesus in you.
To spread the message of His redeeming love, you know what you must do.

Lift up your head and share the story
Of how Jesus died; give Him the glory.

Keep your eyes on Jesus, and be ready to go.
He has overcome the world; the Bible tells us so.

So guard your heart, because we are near the end.
We will soon be with Jesus, our very best friend.

He's our Savior and Lord who gave His life
To deliver us from an eternity of strife.

The Visitor

Around twenty years ago, I took a short-term work assignment in Cambridge, Maryland. I lived there during the week and came home on weekends. One Wednesday night, I decided to attend a Bible study at a nearby church. When I arrived, there was no one there. After a few minutes, a young man in his thirties showed up, who said, "I don't think they are meeting tonight. Would you like to go to the restaurant next door and have a cup of coffee?" I did and we had a great visit that went on for about an hour. While I had never met him before, he seemed to know me as you would know an old friend. During the visit, I began to sense the presence of the Lord in that place. It was one of those moments when my spirit and soul were strengthened as we talked with one another.

At the end of the visit, I asked him what he did for a living. He said that he worked at the local hospital in the radiology department. I asked for his phone number there. He smiled and gave it to me. A couple of days went by, and I decided to give him a call. A pleasant lady answered the radiology department phone, and I asked to speak to my new friend, Del. She said, "I have worked here a number of years and no one by that name has ever worked here." I do not believe my new friend was lying; I believe he may have been an angel assigned to work at that hospital, serving the King of Kings.

The meeting with him was no normal event:
The longer we talked, I knew he'd been sent.

Though we'd never met, he knew me well.
He understood my mind more than I could tell.

This man knew my thoughts, struggles, and fears:
And gave me reasons for hope and good cheer.

As we visited there for over an hour,
I sensed a moving of the Holy Spirit's power.

Before parting that night, we closed in prayer.
It was a divine appointment; I knew God was there.

Two days later, I gave his hospital a call,
And was shocked to learn he'd never worked there at all.

This man who had poured out God's mercy and love
Was an angel in disguise, sent down from above.

The Appointment

In the fall of 2008, I had been struggling with a foot infection that was treated with antibiotics for a period of weeks. Then that infection transitioned into a bacterial infection in my colon, which landed me at the ER. The hospital's initial tests revealed that my body was showing signs of septicemia, and my liver and kidneys were beginning to shut down. Though my heartbeat was erratic, the doctors thought that a less important concern. I was admitted to the ICU, but saw no improvement for the first two days. Then the doctor decided to increase the flow of IV fluids, in the attempt to force my kidneys to work, but that made me feel as if I was about to explode and I passed out. Then I experienced a heavenly appointment.

As I lie there in the hospital bed,
I will never forget what the doctor said.

"Your liver and kidneys are both shutting down,
And signs of septicemia abound."

I was promptly moved to the ICU,
Where they hooked me up to life-saving tubes.

I wasn't getting better in that isolated room,
And soon worries and gloom began to loom.

In misery, I asked God, "Why me?"
But He didn't respond to my pitiful plea.

Instead, He gave me a vision to replace my doubt.
I heard heavenly music begin to swell all around.

I knew I was in the presence of the Lord;
And I hoped my frail life would soon be restored.

At that moment I told Him I was willing to leave,
But I also begged Him to consider a reprieve.

continued

Bruce Goodpaster

It was a feeble plea from a sinner saved by grace,
Because God makes all calls for the human race.

The heavenly music stopped and I was back on earth.
I knew I had been spared for something of more worth.

God touched me, my friend, and extended my days.
For that I am grateful; there's no other phrase.

I made God a promise on that dark, dreary night
To work harder to please Him and walk in the light.

I'm thankful to Jesus for my life that was restored.
I know He loves me and desires that I serve Him as Lord.

His Eye is on the Sparrow

While listening to Larnelle Harris' recording of "His Eye is on the Sparrow", I thought of Jesus' words in Matthew 6 about how God feeds the birds because they don't sow, reap or store their own food. Then in Matthew 10, He reminds his disciples that not even a sparrow falls to the ground without the Father knowing it. Likewise, this hymn reminded me that if God's eye is watching the tiny sparrow, I can be confident that He is also watching over me.

There are times in life when trials come,
And we must trust in Christ; He is the One.

Who sets us free from worry and sin;
When I trust in the Lord, He enters in.

He leads me through the valley, when life gets tough,
And keeps me from stumbling over all that stuff.

He takes away the despair and doubt,
And gives me peace as I travel about.

Why should I complain when He's set me free?
He watches every sparrow and certainly watches me.

Thank you God for the gift of your Son.
His presence in my life is second to none.

I will look to the Lord every moment of the day.
He will deliver me when I ask and pray.

Call out to the Lord when trials rise up in life,
And He will take away the toil and strife.

On the last day we will see Him face to face.
He will welcome us to His Heavenly place.

We will hear the words, "Well done",
And spend eternity with God's only Son.

Shadows

After my mother was diagnosed with brain cancer, she lived only several more months. As I saw this lively, chatty lady rapidly decline, and struggle to articulate her thoughts, my heart longed to speak for her. Though she became but a shadow of her former self, I was thankful for the new body I knew she would soon enjoy.

I walk outside in the bright, sunny day,
But darkness surrounds me and it wants to stay.
I try to speak of the illness that troubles me,
But the words that come out are broken inside, you see.

As my days grow shorter, I struggle even more;
Life, itself, has become quite a chore.
I ask you, God, how long will this battle be,
As the words that come out are broken inside of me.

I look back at my life and have an appreciation
Of God's love for me; I'm a new creation.
I will trust in His strength; He will help me, I know.
As I look for His presence, His love He will show.

And after I leave, I will see Him face to face;
My Father in Heaven who gave me His grace.
Don't feel sorry for me, for my life has been great.
On my very last journey, I don't want to be late.

Welcome

"Welcome, we've been expecting you" was the guard's greeting, as we entered the grounds of the Billy Graham Library in Charlotte, North Carolina. My wife and I were visiting for the first time in 2007, shortly after its opening and one day after my mother had passed away in South Carolina. I couldn't help but think that my mother had just heard those same words herself--in heaven. I felt soothed and comforted, knowing God's plan is perfect.

Welcome, we've been expecting you; it's not by chance you're here.
Your coming is no mistake; it's God's plan, so do not fear.

Relax and enjoy His presence today.
Don't let your thoughts wander and start to stray.

Don't let the problems of the world fill your heart.
They are always seeking to tear you apart.

Simply trust Jesus and you'll find favor with Him.
He is here to help you through thick and thin.

I'm glad you came, my friend; you made the right choice.
As you seek His presence, the angels will rejoice.

Leave your cares and concerns behind you today.
Let Him share them and carry them all away.

As you yield your heart and will to the Lord,
His Holy Spirit will, in you, be out-poured.

May Jesus fill you with peace and His Spirit sweet;
And with confidence that what He began, He will also complete.

Awakened

While I was sleeping one night, I awoke and was overwhelmed by the presence of the Lord. I looked to my left and saw the glory of the Lord. I closed my eyes and opened them again, and He was still there, sitting on His throne! Suddenly, a hand appeared and it was writing in a book. I sensed that He was writing in the Lamb's Book of Life the names of those who were accepting Christ. Then He said, "This is the beginning of the end; I am returning soon."

We can be certain that Christ is our King.
He is returning soon; I can hear the angels sing.

Don't get caught in the world by wasting precious time.
Keep focused on the Lord and listen for the chime.

It's a beautiful melody about the last days we're in,
But you can't hear it when you're wandering in sin.

It will start out with a shout and then a trumpet call.
The saints will meet Jesus in the air; it will be amazing to all.

We must be on the alert; it might even be today,
When the Messiah returns to take us away.

Do you know we are in a battle and the end of days draw near?
But our general is King Jesus, so we have nothing to fear.

As He told me in my vision, the end of days is not far away.
Will you be a soldier for Christ, a ready warrior, today?

Don't worry about tomorrow; He will protect you, my friend.
God will fight your battles; you can expect to win.

Last Days' Dream

On Sunday, December 1, 2013, I dreamed that I had just walked out of church and saw quite a crowd had gathered there. It was a partly cloudy day, and in the distant sky, I saw a pillar of fire. At first, it was somewhat obscured by clouds, so that I could not get a full-scale look. I sensed that God was telling me, "Signs and wonders will precede My coming. Behold My glory. There is work to be done, but I am returning soon." I woke up praising God for His power and promise that He will return to take us home to be with Him.

As I walked out of church, a crowd had gathered about.
We were all in amazement, and some started to shout.

Hanging down from the Heavens was a pillar of fire.
It was shaped in fashion like a large church spire.

As the heavens opened up, God's spirit captured me.
At the top of the pillar was a cross for all to see.

How could this be happening, as some started to cry
While others praised God at the cross hanging high.

We all were in shock; as we looked up again
The cross started bleeding, as Christ died for our sin.

At that very moment, we heard a great voice,
"I gave you My Son; you must make a choice."

He then proclaimed that Christ was returning to Earth.
He's coming in power, and in Him there is worth.

Let's all get ready for the ride of our lives.
When Jesus returns, He will trample all strife.

But time is very short; don't wait any longer.
Trust in Jesus right now, and you will be stronger.

So capture the moment; Christ is here to stay.
Invite Christ into your life and He will never go away.

Signs and Wonders

In July 2014, a missile was headed directly into the heart of Tel Aviv, Israel. The Iron Dome missile intercepting system had missed the target three times, and it was less than a minute until impact. The sirens sounded, but since this was in a heavily populated area, there was no time for everyone to reach the bomb shelters. About thirty seconds before impact, the wind picked up the missile, hurling it into the sea. The Israeli Iron Dome operator who witnessed this event claimed the hand of God had sent the missile into the sea.   Dailymail.co.uk (1)

As the missile approached Tel Aviv that day,
It stirred the hearts of men; all was in disarray.

Who will help us now, as sudden doom draws near?
The future looked dim and all were in great fear.

But the hand of God was moving in the air.
It picked up the missile, with only four seconds to spare.

Yes, the hand of the Lord showed up just in time,
And rescued God's people; it truly was sublime.

When we are put to the test, we, too, must call upon the Lord.
His help is always there, as we walk in one accord.

To live in doubt is really quite absurd.
We must always call on God; it's written in His word.

Our ideas seem better, and we think we know what to do,
But when His blessings come down, He makes all things new.

The next time you think you know what you should do,
Start by calling on God, and He will lead you, too.

---

1. Reilly, Jill. " 'Hand of God' prevents rocket from striking its target: Israeli Iron Dome operator says sudden gust of wind blew missile into sea when defense system failed." Dailymail.co.uk, 6 August 2014. Accessed 3 May 2017.

Holy Spirit

My younger brother had been in ill health for a number of months, but his death caught me off guard, and I struggled to make sense of it. A few days after hearing it, I noticed a lone egret on the pond near our house which reminded me of the dove that had been present at Jesus' baptism. I felt it was God's sign that His Holy Spirit would be with me and carry me through my sadness.

My spirit was heavy, and I could not sleep.
My heart ached within me, and I started to weep.

As I was driving that day, I saw a beautiful sight.
It was an egret on the pond; what a huge delight.

In that very same moment, God's Spirit stirred my soul.
He whispered to me, softly, "My Presence will make you whole."

"I sent you the egret to remind you that I'm still here.
I've sent you the Holy Spirit; you don't have to fear."

Several days passed, as I traveled far away.
God's presence was still in me, each and every day.

On the third day of my journey, God spoke to me, once more,
When I found an egret feather on the knob of my hotel door.

God had sent the feather to make sure I would stay on course;
To keep me from wandering and falling into deep remorse.

If you think for one moment you can make it on your own,
You will soon find out that you are not alone.

Look up to Jesus; He's your very best friend.
He will lift you up and carry you to the end.

Keep your eyes fixed on Jesus; He is the only way.
You will enter His presence on the final day.

Jesus, Our Ark of Safety

*In the mountains of Western Maryland, there is an unfinished replica of
the ark visible from Interstate 68. I've noticed it often when driving by,
looking for signs of progress. Recently, I had a dream in which I saw this
ark and a large cross erected in front of it. Though the ark is still unfin-
ished, Christ's work on the cross is finished. Perhaps one day before Jesus
returns, this ark project will also be finished.*

When the world was young and its people wicked,
God looked for one righteous and found Noah beloved.

He told him to build an ark of safety that was huge,
To preserve his family and some animals from the coming deluge.

After the flood came and went, the ark landed on Mount Ararat,(2)
Where all disembarked and thanked God for their new habitat.

Some consider this only a legend about a boat no one could make,
But some have scaled the mount, claiming remains that don't seem
fake.

The day will come when all the world will confess
Noah's ark provided salvation and freedom to rest.

Today, Jesus is our ark of safety and salvation.
Have you met Him and trusted Him without reservation?

He dwelled among us and lived a life sinless and unselfish.
When He died on the cross, His work was finished.

Don't wait another moment to receive Jesus as your savior.
After you have trusted Him as Lord, you will have favor.

Call upon Him to be your ark of safety and salvation.
He will redeem and give you restoration.

---

2. Genesis 8:4

A Pivot Point in History

The days are getting shorter, but we have nothing to fear.
Just don't look through life in the rearview mirror.

Yes, there are wars of desolation; it's very plain to see.
And I would call this a pivot point in history.

The forces of good and evil are obviously all around;
Yet, as we walk with Jesus, we will gain more ground.

As warriors for Christ, we must call upon the Lord.
He will quickly arrive with His powerful, two-edged sword.

As we read the Word of God, it will always give us hope.
It will help us overcome life's very slippery slope.

Don't ever give up when the chips are down.
God has His eye on you, and there are angels all around.

Yes, we can make a difference, as we trust in Christ our Lord.
He will truly bless us, as we walk in one accord.

May He bless you, my friend, as you call out to Him and pray.
He always listens, and He knows what you're going to say.

Don't look to the left or right; just walk by faith and not by sight.
Keep your eyes on Jesus, and you'll overcome any plight.

Open Your Heart

God Is Not Dead

When I look at the stars that are hung in place,
It reminds me of the Creator of the human race.

Yes, God is alive and you can find Him everywhere.
He is our Alpha and Omega; He truly does care.

After a steady rainfall, we see Him in the sky,
As we stare in wonder at the rainbow up high.

As we look at the mountains, how majestic they are.
It's a wonder to behold, as you approach them in your car.

And when you reach the top, you see the valley below;
The beauty of the meadows and towns all aglow.

No, nothing happened by chance; it was created by our Lord.
He rules over heaven and earth, the One whom we love and adore.

And He's returning soon to rule and reign down here.
Are you ready to meet Him? Someday He will appear.

His plans are for good and He has a plan, it's true.
Or, are you too proud to meet Him? He's watching over you.

Please trust in Jesus; He's calling out to you, my friend.
Our days are getting shorter; we have an expected end.

Are you ready to trust in Christ as your Lord?
Place your trust in Him today and walk in one accord.

Yes, Jesus is calling out; can you hear His gentle voice?
When you trust in Him as your Savior, the angels will rejoice.

God's Greatest Gift

Christ came to the world as a baby in a manger.
He left Heaven to live in a world filled with danger.

He had a humble beginning for One who was a King.
It was part of God's design; He reigns over everything.

At the time of His birth, all power was in Rome.
Jesus was from a higher place, as Heaven was his home.

He never led an army or had a noble title.
He was a lowly carpenter, and He was never idle.

When He was thirty, His ministry began.
He spread good news throughout the land.

His message was of mercy, truth, and love:
Gifts sent down from our Father above

But the greatest gift was when Jesus died on a cross.
Our life's dearest gain came at His life's loss.

It was a moment in time when Jesus hung on that tree.
While suffering and bleeding, He died for you and me.

Many thought that all hope left when He lay in the tomb.
He was dead in the grave; it all pointed to doom.

In the twinkling of an eye, God's plan fell into place.
Jesus broke out of the grave, defying time and space.

But Christ is coming back in glory and power.
You might even say it will be His finest hour.

Have you trusted in the Lord? The day is drawing near.
He has promised to return, and all will see Him appear.

T.G.I.F.

Every day is T.G.I.F. for me:
Thank God I'm Forgiven is plain to see.

Before I knew Jesus, I wandered around,
And often found myself lying alone on the ground.

My hope was in friends and exciting things to do,
But at the end of the day, I met my Waterloo.

Without Jesus in my heart, I was all alone.
It was an empty feeling, like that of a stone.

But God kept knocking on the door of my heart.
I asked Him in, and He gave me a fresh start.

Yes, Jesus died for my sins and He set me free.
I asked for forgiveness; He heard my plea.

Don't waste another day without asking Him in.
Call on Him now; He will forgive your sin.

Then every day will be a T.G.I.F. for you.
Receive Him as your savior; that's what you need to do.

When God Shows Up

Two thousand years ago, many witnessed His birth.
He lived among us on the great planet Earth.

It was Jesus who came for every tribe, tongue, and nation.
He paid for my sins, and I'm a new creation.

Jesus taught us how to live in a world full of strife.
He died for my sins, and He gave up His life.

There's a stirring in my soul; could it be a revival?
I want to be ready for the Savior's arrival.

Jesus foretold that the last days would be here.
It's time to repent and stop living in fear.

No one knows the day, but He has a schedule to keep.
He might even return while we are asleep.

God's Son will show up; are you ready to go?
Have you made a decision? Is the answer still no?

For many days and nights, I've been unable to sleep.
I made a promise to God, and one I will keep.

He told me to tell others what He's going to do.
Don't wait another day; He gave His life for you.

Yes, there's a stirring in my soul, and it won't go away.
You must make up your mind and receive Jesus today.

Expectation

Are you ready for the battle that we see most every day?
We are drawing near the time when we will fly away.

The day is drawing near when we will see Jesus appear.
He will take us to a place that is safer than down here.

For down here there's travail; times of trial and of trouble.
God foretold years ago of this suffering and resulting rubble.

Those days have finally come, as prophesied long ago.
There are wars and rumors of wars, as we travel to and fro.

But don't throw in the towel; there is hope for everyone.
You must trust in Jesus Christ; He is God's only Son.

He left the glory of heaven to live down here awhile.
Jesus was a servant to all; He went the extra mile.

That mile took Him to Calvary, where He was crucified on a tree.
As He died on the cross, His love was plain to see.

He said, "Father, forgive them; they know not what they do."
This was an act of love; yes, He even died for you.

Don't wait any longer to receive Jesus as your savior.
As you trust in Him, my friend, in Him you will find favor.

Hope or Despair

Each day is filled with hope or despair.
We find ourselves living with people who don't care.

It seems that many folks have forgotten how to smile.
Life's struggles can make any of us ponder for a while.

But just when I start thinking that my world is in disarray,
I'm reminded of what God told me on a dark and gloomy day.

Yes, His plans for me are good, and He loves me without reservation.
The Lord loves everyone of every race, tribe, and nation.

What a price was paid to give hope to everyone.
It was God's greatest gift; Jesus Christ, His only Son.

Yes, He was crucified on a cross to pay the penalty for our sin.
He even said, "Father, forgive them," and died so that we might win.

God gave us hope when Jesus bled and died on the cross.
If this had not happened, we would suffer eternal loss.

Yes, we must confess our sin to the Lord above,
And then He will welcome us in with great joy and love.

Eternity is a gift, but God paid a great price.
It was Christ's death at Calvary; God was very precise.

Each person must decide where to spend eternity.
Will you trust in Jesus or drown in despair's sea?

Yes, we live in a world filled with hope and despair.
Trust in Jesus, my friend; He loves you and cares.

His Eyes Are Watching Over You

When an eagle looks down from his lofty view,
He sees God's creation differently than we do.

The eagle's eyes are sharper than the common man's,
And the eagle flies higher than any human can.

But the Lord of heaven and of earth can see everything.
So what can we give Him; what can we bring?

What can we give to the One who created us all?
We pale in His presence; I can hear Him call.

He knows my name and each person down here.
He is watching over us; we have nothing to fear.

Trusting in yourself will leave you in an empty place.
After all is said and done, you will see His face.

I'm talking about the Father who is looking down in love.
Yes, He gave His son Jesus as a gift from above.

To die for our sins on a cross at Calvary,
He paid a dear price for all of us to be free.

Look up to God in heaven and repent of sin today.
He will hear you cry and take your sin away.

There's No One Like Jehovah

We meet the Lord with great anticipation.
He is always there in every situation.

God's Spirit is pouring out among all the people.
Don't just look for Him in a building with a steeple.

We are in the last days, and He has promised to return.
As time passes by, many refuse to learn.

Where are you, my friend, in your journey through life?
Do you have a nice home and a happy wife?

Or, are you missing the mark at the end of the day?
Many travel the wide path, and it's a dear price they'll pay.

The only lasting hope is in Jehovah God, our Lord.
He meets our needs and carries a two-edged sword.

The sword is God's Word; we call it the Bible.
It encourages our hearts as we read of His arrival.

He's coming back soon to take us all home.
We will be in His presence; we are never alone.

The Promise

God has promised that He will never leave or forsake us;
And when it's our time to go home, we won't miss the bus.

Jesus will come down riding on a cloud.
We will hear a trumpet sound that's certain to be loud.

It will be a great reunion the day we meet the King.
Make no mistake about it; He is over everything.

Those who don't trust Jesus are on a different path.
They will be under judgment and will incur God's wrath.

Accepting Jesus as your savior is really up to you.
It's totally your decision; do you know what you will do?

If for now you have rejected Him, don't put this off too long.
Rejecting Him is not the answer; it will only turn out wrong.

Reach out to Jesus and receive Him today.
Accept Him now into your heart, and He'll come in to stay.

Yes, Jesus is coming back and His promises are true.
He knows your name and has done His part; the rest is up to you.

God's Clock

The world's on a time clock
That's moving quite fast.

It's moving very quickly;
How much longer will things last?

That's why we need to stop
And call upon the Lord.

He's the One who runs the clock.
He will never be ignored.

We have placed our hopes in the perfect plan
That God designed for every man.

But we had to leave the Garden one day,
As we disobeyed God and He sent us away.

He didn't forsake us and leave us down here.
He sent us His Son--baby Jesus came here.

His life was cut short, and He suffered great strife.
Yes, He paid for our sins and gave up His life.

Where are you on God's time clock; have you called out to Him?
Did you know that He loves you, and life's not a whim?

So call out to Jesus and receive Him today.
He died for your sins; what more can I say?

You are never alone, not one moment; it's true.
Don't resist Him anymore; you know what you must do.

Receive Christ as your Lord and your Savior,
And find, in Him, an abundance of favor.

We Will Meet Him Face to Face

He's coming soon; are you ready, my friend?
You may not know it, but we are near the end.

It's the end of this world, as we know it, here.
But if you trust in Jesus, you have nothing to fear.

This world's full of darkness, and sin all around.
Our hope is in Jesus, where we stand on solid ground.

If you are struggling with life, and you live in despair,
Cast your hope on King Jesus. He's the One who will care

When I call out to Him, He will listen to me.
He gives peace; lean closely to Him; His presence you'll see.

Each day is a challenge; we need His help, and for this I pray.
Once you've trusted in Jesus, He's only a prayer away.

When I am at my weakest and have no place to go,
I look up to Jesus; He overcomes any foe.

Just pray and read the Bible, and listen to His voice.
Yes, He's that close; it will make you rejoice.

It's almost time to go to that celestial place,
Where we will see Jesus; we'll meet Him face to face!

Walk With Him

All Things Become New

Each day of life is a blessing from God.
He has given us hope, as we live on this sod.

The world reaches out to our hearts every day,
But we who know the Lord must kneel down and pray.

It is God who hears our prayers; He has given us favor.
We've placed our trust in Him; He's our Lord and Savior.

God will never forsake us as we live down here.
His mighty plan is at work; we have nothing to fear.

Keep your hopes set on Him; avoid all worldly pleasure.
Look up to Him; He's our heavenly treasure.

The world will fade away, when we live with Him in glory.
King Jesus will soon return; it's a never-ending story.

Keep trusting in the Lord, as your future is bright.
He's coming in power, and He will make all things right.

Remember, my friend, God is watching over you.
Trust in Christ as your Savior; He will make all things new.

Vision

When I start my day, I must look up to the Lord.
He is my hope, the One I adore.

A prayer in the morning is what I need most.
As I yield my will to Him, it's in Jesus I boast.

Keeping my eyes on the Lord is an important part;
With Him helping me, as I give Him my heart.

Jesus is there; He is there to stay.
It's me who sometimes heads out in the wrong way.

What can I do if I head out on my own?
It's a troubling outcome when I'm all alone.

Listen closely to the Lord as you start your day,
And you can be sure He will direct your way.

Keep your eyes fixed on Jesus, for He is the light.
As we submit to Him, our futures will be bright.

We are only down here awhile in this earthly place,
But eternity is in Heaven, where we see Him face to face.

Look all around; the days are fading away, my friend.
Keep your eyes turned to Jesus; it's not the end.

He's coming back to redeem us from this place.
Are you ready to meet Him and see Him face to face?

Calling on the Lord

Thank you, Lord, for your plans for my life,
As I live in a world filled with evil and strife.

You knew all about me before I was born,
And watched over me while I was lost and forlorn.

Again, I thank you for giving me hope;
Making my future positive and helping me to cope.

With problems all around us, it's upon You we call
Your plans are perfect, and You are the Lord of all.

When we call upon You with all of our hearts.
You listen to us and make the waters part.

As I think about those times that I wandered far from You,
You remind me that Jesus said, "They know not what they do".

That's when You lift us up from the pit of miry clay,
And forgive our sins, starting the dawn of a new day.

Our footsteps are firm, as You put them on solid ground,
And every place we go, we see You all around.

The next time you encounter any trials or tribulations,
Call out to the Lord, who is over all the nations.

Our hope is in Jesus, as we live on the earth.
He has all the answers and in Him, there is worth.

Faith

We must place our faith in Christ, our Lord,
And walk with Him in one accord.

We walk by faith and not by sight,
And He will lead us to do what's right.

Our hope in Jesus is an awesome treasure.
His blessings come down beyond all measure.

As you call upon Jesus, and trust Him today,
His Spirit will lead as you call out and pray.

Don't let worry and trouble bother you.
Lean upon the Savior; He will show you what to do.

Yes, we have many struggles as we live down here,
But our real home is in heaven, and that's very clear.

We are only vapors here for a short while.
Remembering our eternal home should always make us smile.

Don't listen to the devil; he only has bad news.
Keep your eyes on Jesus, and you will never lose.

The troubles of this world will soon fade away.
Let the light of Christ lead you on each and every day.

Finding Favor With God

Each day is filled with toil and trouble.
How do you deal with it, when you are in the rubble?

Do you say "woe is me" and stumble about,
Or do you call out to the Lord with a mighty shout?

It's not always easy to submit to the Lord,
To trust in His goodness and final reward.

As you read God's Word, He will lead you each day.
Walking closely beside Him and you'll never go astray.

It says in God's Word that He will lift you up,
From the pit of miry clay where your feet are stuck.

When He firmly sets your feet on solid ground,
Stay fastened to the Rock while you're earthbound.

God's angels are watching over everything you do.
When you're led by the Father, He gives hope to you.

As you begin each day, yield it to the Lord in prayer.
Wear His easy yoke and give Him your burdens to bear.

Don't forget that Jesus delights to give you favor.
His love is unconditional and will never waiver.

I Found It

Have you ever misplaced an item and couldn't find it anywhere?
You searched all over the house, and it wasn't even there.

Even worse, you start to worry and your imagination kicks in.
You start feeling desperate and call your next of kin.

For many of us, we ask our spouses and they have something to say.
Do you remember where you left it when you had it yesterday?

Of course, I don't, but thanks a lot; you are a lot of help.
Your frustration only escalates and you start to moan and whelp.

Then, you finally find it in the living room and ask the infamous question:
"Did you find it and leave it there?" I'm getting indigestion.

Do you search for life's answers in struggles that arise each day?
Or, do you act out toward others and put things in disarray?

The next time you're missing something and at your wit's end,
Ask God to help you out; He is your very best friend.

Don't look to the left or look to the right, as you search around the house.
Just look to Jesus and ask for His help; don't take it out on your spouse!

Found Faithful

From an early age, Jesus was faithful to the Lord;
Doing temple business at age twelve for the Father He adored.

His vision and message were seen clearly in His life.
He lived among us to pay for our sins and end our strife.

He healed the blind and made crooked legs walk.
Though He was God in the flesh, some still balked.

He was despised and rejected by those He came to love;
While hanging on the cross, even forsaken by His Father above.

He said, "Father, forgive them for doing this to me."
"They know not what they do. They're blind and cannot see."

Instead of calling ten thousand angels to intervene and set Him free,
He chose to suffer and die in a place called Calvary.

Once you trust Jesus as your Lord and Savior,
There will be a major change in your behavior.

You will have a desire to be found faithful to the Lord;
And one day, you will see Him and receive your reward.

What greater reward than to have life eternal with our King?
We will see Him face to face and hear the angels sing.

Follow the Lord

If we listen to the Lord, we will hear His voice.
We will find it easy to make the right choice.

If we go our own way down the wide and traveled path,
We will find ourselves entering a route that's filled with wrath.

We must never forget that God's promises are true.
As we call to Him for help, He will show us what to do.

Yes, sometimes we have problems that cause us all to doubt:
But when we call upon the Lord, the enemy will go out.

The Lord will set our feet on solid ground.
His righteousness will reign in the world all around.

So call out to the Lord, and you will see,
That His love and power will set you free.

Start your day crying out to the Lord,
And He will help you walk in one accord.

One day, you will awake and meet Him face to face.
It's where we want to be in His glory and His grace.

Looking Up To Jesus

The world is filled with toil and tribulation.
We even find ourselves in irreversible situations.

It is at this juncture we must call upon the Lord.
For in Him we find peace; He carries a mighty sword.

When I find myself fighting battles on my own,
I only wind up realizing that I am all alone.

It's easy to go down the road that most others choose.
After all, we think many are on this road; how can we lose?

As I turn the corner, moving at a hundred miles per hour,
Heading in the wrong direction, I call to a higher power.

Then suddenly, God shows up and takes control:
Filling me with His presence; the One who makes me whole.

Yes, Jesus is the one who calms the sea within.
His overwhelming power and love conquers and always wins.

If you feel backed into a corner, with nowhere to turn,
Shout out to the Lord, and the enemy will flee and burn.

We see the day coming when Jesus will appear.
Walk closely to Him and your future will be clear.

Meditate and Activate

When I read God's Word, I listen for His voice.
When He speaks to me, there is no other choice.

He breaks down the walls of my wayward heart,
And gives me new hope and a fresh start.

Put aside those habits that lead us all astray.
Just call on the Lord, and He will show you the way.

Jesus is the best friend that you will ever know.
He will lead and guide you in the way you should go.

We must strive to read God's Word every day;
There, we find a close friend who leads our way.

As you read God's Word and submit to Him each day,
You will learn to walk by faith and to pray.

Lift up your voice and give praise to our Lord.
He will hear your cry, as you walk in one accord.

Your quiet strength grows, as you call out in prayer.
It will flourish because He really does care.

Walking By Faith

If you read God's Word, He will bless you everyday.
He is always faithful, despite what others say.

When you think of Abraham, he was one who believed.
When God tested Him, he was not deceived.

Do you ask the Lord to lead you every day?
Or, do you walk on your own, without knowing His way?

Don't think that on your own you can meet challenges that arise,
Because acting in your own strength may serve Satan in disguise.

What may appear to be right might turn out to be wrong.
You must call out to Jesus and listen for His song.

His song calls us to serve Him and always be a blessing.
If we follow a different path, we are just second-guessing.

It's my prayer, my friend, that you be faithful to the end.
Just keep looking to Jesus, as you travel around that bend.

Walking by faith instead of by sight, doing what is right:
Never giving up and always fighting the good fight.

Those who are found faithful will be rewarded on high.
We will hear God say, "Well done" in the sweet bye-and-bye.

Standing in His Presence

Who may ascend into the hill of the Lord? Or who may stand in His holy
place? He who has clean hands and a pure heart.

Psalm 24:3,4a

Who may ascend into the presence of God?
Only those who trust in Jesus may walk on holy sod.

He is the One who gives hope everyday.
We must listen to His voice and not walk away.

As we stand in His presence, we begin to understand
That for each one who knows Him, He has a master plan.

We want to be the generation that always seeks Your face.
You are our mighty God who hung the stars in place.

There should be nothing down here that we need to fear.
When we pray and ask our Lord, He will surely draw near.

My day always goes better when I begin it with prayer.
My God is always listening; He is the One who cares.

And there will be a day when we leave this earthly place,
Joining up with Christ our Savior; we will see His face.

But until that day arrives, keep looking to God in prayer,
Because He is always listening; He is everywhere.

The Journey to the Top

Have you been to the mountaintop in your search for God?
It's not an easy ascent, climbing where only a few have trod.

You must travel a narrow path to reach the mountain peak.
It takes a humble heart; one that is stout, yet meek.

You may begin your journey from a dark and dreary place,
But it is worth the effort as you run in the great race.

Many may try to mislead you to a different path that is bleak,
But you must follow Jesus to find the answers you seek.

Your guiding light is Jesus, who helps you along the way.
Listen closely to His voice; He will guide you every day.

May God reward you as you seek Him out.
Don't give up early, or try another route.

Keep your eyes focused on Jesus while running this race.
When you reach the mountaintop, you will see His glorious face.

Glimpses of Heaven

Have you ever seen the sunrise at the beginning of a day;
Watched the sunbeams shining through clouds in fine array?

And what about the sunset as daylight starts to fade,
Contrasting colors cavorting in a beautiful parade?

The starry skies at night display a beauty all their own.
We're amazed at the heavenly sight and know we're not alone.

There's a Master Designer who created everything.
He's always been present; it's His praises we sing.

From the smallest newborn babe to the towering redwood trees,
His designs are flawless and created with ease.

Yes, we get a glimpse of heaven each day we live down here.
He fills each step with hope and takes away our fear.

A Planting of the Lord

Our only hope is in Jesus, our Savior and Lord.
He is the One we need, as we walk in one accord.

He has opened and closed doors, as we seek to do His will.
It's by His Spirit we are led, as He abides with us still.

We call on You today, as we plant a brand new work.
A place where people will find Jesus; this is no quirk.

We ask for Your blessing as we start out today,
And we will glorify Him, as He is the only way.

You are our source and our hope in this life.
Please lead us, O Lord, and deliver us from strife.

As we worship You and call out Your name,
We ask for Your blessing and, in Jesus' name, proclaim.

May the power of your Holy Spirit fill this place.
We ask You to lead us, as we reach the human race.

We thank you, Lord, for your presence today.
Please lead us and guide us, as we walk the narrow way.

The Silent Voice

I'm alive and safe in my mother's womb,
But I'm hearing troubled voices now.
Will this womb become my tomb?
It's overwhelming to think that my tiny life may end;
Isn't there a God who has created me?

I am crying now, but you can't hear me, my friend.
I'm not a fetus or a parasite.
I am your first child; don't let my life end.
I think I hear my grandparents,
Who are telling you what you must do.
Please listen carefully to them,
They want me to live; it's true.

I am a little light, part of God's creation.
Don't snuff me out and throw me away.
My life is precious, filled with joy and anticipation.
I'm praying now that you will do the right thing,
And when you choose life, the angels will sing!

The Rushing Wind

The wind is a force that we cannot see,
And the power it pours out is amazing to me.

The wind, in its fury, can topple a tree,
Or upend a house and make us all flee.

The sun gives us warmth that we all need,
But the wind cools things down, yes indeed.

Have you ever seen a fire roaring out of control,
Fanned by the wind that is on a roll?

Late at night, we are awakened by a strong, rushing wind,
Which gives us a rush and frightens us within.

We pale at the power that the wind displays,
But when the wind and rain subside, it becomes a sunny day.

And then we see a rainbow appear,
Letting us know we have nothing to fear.

Stepping outside, we feel a gentle breeze
And sense the peace, which puts us at ease.

Trumpet
Sounds

Awake America

Our nation is in a struggle, this land of the free and home of the brave.
The direction we are headed seems beyond any that one could save.

Can you hear the rumors of wars thundering throughout the
world today?
No, America is not immune to them; the struggle is heading our way.

We all remember 9/11, a day of tragedy that struck our great land.
It created such fear and tragedy among us; we could hardly stand.

To think of all those lives that were lost, in such short duration;
"Where is America," we cried, while the enemy had a celebration.

To think in our country that ISIS may attack is certain humiliation.
What can we do to avoid a trap of possible annihilation?

Our only hope is in the Lord; He is the One who carries a sword.
We must submit to our God, the One we adore.

Allowing Him to take over is a total act of submission.
It's not a natural choice; it's quite a different rendition.

We must fall on our knees and cry out to God.
He will hear our cries, as we struggle on this sod.

He will lift us with wings like eagles, casting down our adversary.
It's plain to see that God's power is here to give us the victory.

We must humble ourselves through the night until that exciting day
When Jesus returns and gives us hope, no matter what men may say.

We must trust and submit to the Lord, and ask Him to intervene
That He may dwell in our hearts and in our land; a picture so serene.

Last Days' Struggle

As we hear of terror in a distant land,
It saddens and reminds us we must take a stand.

Why are these things happening and our world in disarray?
We're in the last days, and it's not going away.

'Twas foretold in God's Word, two thousand years ago,
As the future unfolds, we see our mighty foe.

We must look to the Lord, the Creator of earth,
Who knows our names even before our births.

He will overcome evil and replace it with good,
Bringing peace to the world as He said He would.

Don't let fear rule your heart in the days ahead.
Look to the Lord to watch over you instead.

Yes, things may get worse before they get better,
But Satan's days are numbered and the evil he unfetters.

Keep your eyes on the Lord; He will give you peace.
The closer we walk with Him, the more our fears will cease

He promises to come back and bring peace to all.
Place your trust in Jesus and answer His call.

The Eye of the Storm

In the world, you will find that we have tribulation.
It covers the Earth to every tribe and every nation.

When we arise everyday,
We must call on God and pray.

For He gives us hope in every situation,
And He gives us peace; it's a great revelation.

In the eye of the storm,
You will find Jesus our Lord.

We can trust in God's Word.
It's sharper than any sword.

Yes, there is peace for all men,
It is available today.

You will find it in God's Word,
And also when you pray.

Do you sense the eyes of the Lord?
They move over all the Earth.

He is watching over us,
And in Him, there's new birth.

We are in the last days; the signs will not waiver.
You must reach out to Jesus, in whom you will find favor.

Call upon the Lord now, because He's watching over you.
He's the answer to our troubles; you know what you must do.

The eyes of the Lord cover the Earth.
Give Him your heart, for in Him there is worth.

The Clock is Ticking

As we look around the world, we see toil and trouble.
With all the conflict about, we see cities in rubble.

There are fires in our homeland that continue to spread.
Many have lost their homes and can't get ahead.

Nation arises against nation on a very high scale.
It's no wonder fear grows, as they see leaders fail.

And where is America in this struggle, we see?
We seem to have failed in our hope to remain free.

Will our homeland be invaded? May it never be;
We must remain strong; this is my plea.

Did you know these things have been foretold?
This is not a mystery, God wants us to know.

Yes, it's written in the Bible that this would all take place.
Don't be too hasty while in this life's race.

We see through the glass darkly, as we live down here.
But when Jesus returns, all things will be clear.

Life's clock is ticking; it will not be slow.
When Jesus returns, will you be ready to go?

Where Am I?

I was standing at the gas pump on a bright and sunny day,
When suddenly I heard a trumpet and all was in disarray.

The man who had been beside me was nowhere to be seen.
The nozzle was lying on the ground; what did this all mean?

I had heard about the Rapture--had this event taken place?
Where have all the people gone, someplace in outer space?

I got out my big, leather Bible and read these words from there.
It said that when the trumpet blew, we'd vanish in the air.

Then I called some friends, but they didn't answer the phone.
Had they left me, too? I began to feel all alone.

My wife was out of town, so I called her up, too.
No answer there; what in the world could I do?

I heard another sound and opened up my eyes.
God had put me in a dream; what a wonderful surprise.

I called out to Him and confessed my sin.
Jesus heard my prayer and took me in.

If you don't know Jesus, reach out to Him today.
Become part of God's family without any further delay.

For What It Was Worth

'Twas the night before the Rapture and all through the Earth,
All the people were stirring, for what it was worth.
As dawn was drawing near, I looked up into the sky,
And there was King Jesus, on a cloud riding high.
The sound of a trumpet was heard everywhere.
When all of a sudden, I was swooped up into the air.
Great joy filled my heart, as I headed toward my Lord.
He had kept His promise; we were all in one accord.
Then, a thought came to mind as we started to depart.
Many friends were not with me, and it saddened my heart.
Then I heard Jesus proclaim, as we left Planet Earth,
"Everyone else was too busy for what it was worth."

When Jesus died on the cross, He poured out His love,
And He's coming back in great power from above.
Take a moment right now and consider the cost.
Jesus died for your sins on a rugged, old cross.
His plans are for good, if you trust Him today.
Take a moment right now and don't linger--pray.
Receive Him right now; don't keep wasting away.
True freedom is in Jesus, and in that there is worth.
Then you will be ready to leave Planet Earth.

Are You Ready?

Are you ready for that moment when your life on Earth will end?
We are getting close; please listen to me, my friend.

God's perfect plan was put in place two thousand years ago.
He sent His Son to die for us, because He loved us so.

He won't be late when He returns; will you be there on time?
The Lord's in control, so look to Him; can't you hear the chime?

Can you hear the clock ticking? It's a sign to all.
When you hear the trumpet blow, get ready for the call.

But if it blows and you've rejected Him, my friend,
Then you will face the wrath of God and all hope for you will end.

Jesus is coming back, and time has slipped away
Because those who reject the Savior are headed for Judgment Day.

Just call on Jesus; don't wait another hour.
He will forgive your sin, and you will sense His power.

In the Twinkling of an Eye

Behold I tell you a mystery: We shall not all sleep, but we shall all be changed, in a moment, in the twinkling of an eye, at the last trumpet. For the trumpet will sound, and the dead will be raised incorruptible, and we shall be changed.

I Corinthians 15:51,52

In the twinkling of an eye, we will leave this lowly place.
As we head up in the clouds, we will meet Him face to face.

Never let your fears down here consume your days on Earth;
Rather, think of Christ, because in Him there is great worth.

He left the portals of heaven to give peace to men's hearts.
Once you trust in Jesus, you have a brand new start.

Tonight, before you retire and head off to bed,
Take a moment to go outside and search the stars overhead.

As you wonder at the glory of the stars displayed above,
Give your thanks to the Creator, the God of endless love.

The beauty of the stars contrasts Christ's death on Calvary,
Where He hung upon that cross and died for you and me.

I ask you again, don't let your fears rule your heart today.
Just trust in Christ and they will go away.

Please call upon the King of Kings, and He will hear your voice.
He will give you the strength you need and a reason to rejoice.

And when your last day on earth is done,
You will be face to face with the Holy One.

The Sound of the Trumpet

There's a new world coming, and it won't be very long.
There's no time for weakness; we must remain strong.

If you think you know the answer, you may be in for a shock,
Because our hope is in Jesus Christ, who is our solid rock.

The examples He gave us were of patience and of love.
He surrendered His life to the Father above.

This was God's only Son, who redeemed us from our fate.
Jesus bled and He died for our sins, which were great.

Even in His last breath, as Jesus hung on that tree,
He said, "Forgive them, oh Father," and died for you and me.

At that very moment, Jesus paid a great price.
Our sins were forgiven, as He gave up His life.

Every day in this world, there's a choice we must make.
Have you trusted in Jesus, or have you decided to wait?

God's clock keeps ticking, as the day draws near
When that trumpet will sound and the whole world will hear.

Will you be ready to meet Him when that day finally comes,
Or will you stand on your own and twiddle your thumbs?

Have you considered the Lord who hung the stars in place?
The next time He shows up, all will see His face.

He will return in a moment, in the twinkling of an eye.
Those who have trusted in Him will go to heaven on high.

continued

But those who are left will remember the trumpet call,
Because they had a chance but forsook it all.

Take a moment right now and ask Jesus to come in.
He will give you hope and forgive you of your sin.

God is the Creator of life, and you need to call on Him today.
He will forgive you of your sins and they will be washed away.

The Rising of the Son

Many years have passed since the rising of the Son,
And now He's coming back to be seen by everyone.

I'm talking about the King of Kings, the Lord of heaven and earth.
His name is Jesus; He was destined from His birth.

He'll be coming in the sky for all the world to see.
They will marvel at this glorious sight of the Lamb of Calvary.

Just as He promised, His words are true:
The One who died for me and for you.

He's coming back in His might and power.
It will be the world's finest hour.

There are many who question the return of the Son,
But He's coming back; God's chosen One.

You may wake up one day at the appointed hour,
When Jesus comes back in His might and power.

You will know at that time that the prophecy was true:
That King Jesus is Lord, the One who died for you.

It's now up to you; you must make a choice.
Ask Jesus to come in, and the angels will rejoice.

It's the most important decision that you will ever make:
To reject Him now would be a huge mistake.

So call upon Jesus and flee the human race.
Your reward will be heaven, where you'll see Him face to face.

What If

What if Jesus came back in the very next hour:
In all of His glory, majesty, and power?

Are you ready to meet Him this very day?
He's coming back soon; He won't go away.

And if you're not ready, it won't go well.
Trust in Jesus now to stay out of hell.

I can promise you, friend, that He'll soon return.
It's up to you now, or would you rather burn?

Just confess your sin and call on Him, my friend,
And He will save your soul; His power will come in.

So don't waste another minute; call out to His name.
He will change your life; you won't be the same.

Yes, He's coming back, maybe in the next hour.
You must trust in Jesus, our mighty and strong tower.

CPSIA information can be obtained
at www.ICGtesting.com
Printed in the USA
BVOW07s1408250617
487639BV00004B/13/P